FANTASY

FOR OBOE, B-FLAT CLARINET, AND PIANO
BY CHRISTOS TSITSAROS

ISBN 978-1-4950-8442-3

7777 W. BLUEMOUND RD. P.O. BOX 13819 MILWAUKEE, WI 53213

In Australia Contact:
Hal Leonard Australia Pty. Ltd.
4 Lentara Court
Cheltenham, Victoria, 3192 Australia
Email: ausadmin@halleonard.com.au

No part of this publication may be reproduced in any form or by any means without the prior written permission of the Publisher.

Visit Hal Leonard Online at
www.halleonard.com

CONTENTS

PIANO SCORE.............................4

OBOE PART................................28

CLARINET PART 34

FANTASY

By CHRISTOS TSITSAROS

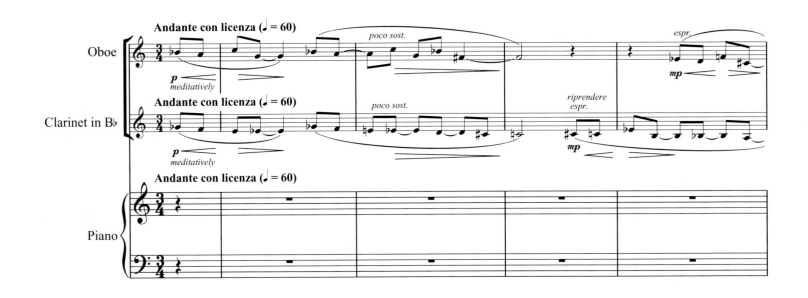

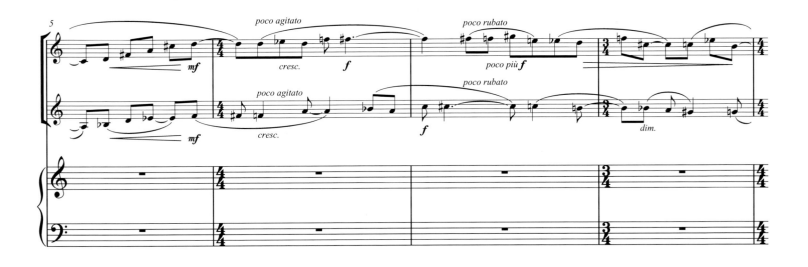

Copyright © 2017 by HAL LEONARD LLC
International Copyright Secured   All Rights Reserved

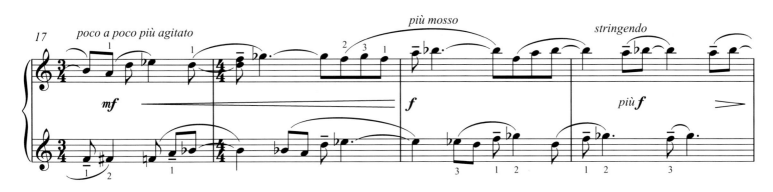

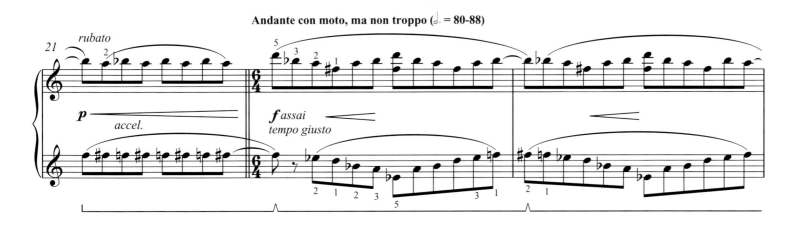

Andante con moto, ma non troppo (♩. = 80-88)

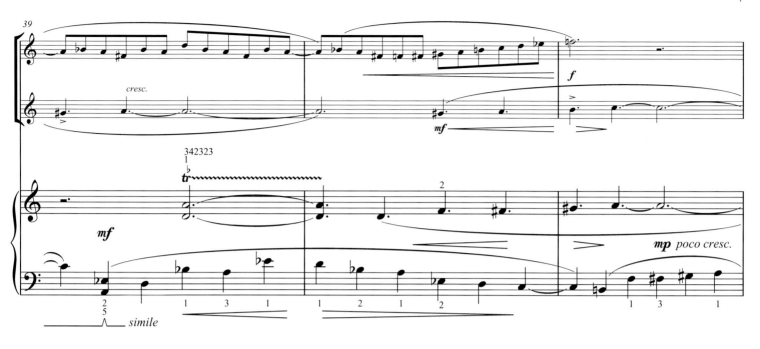

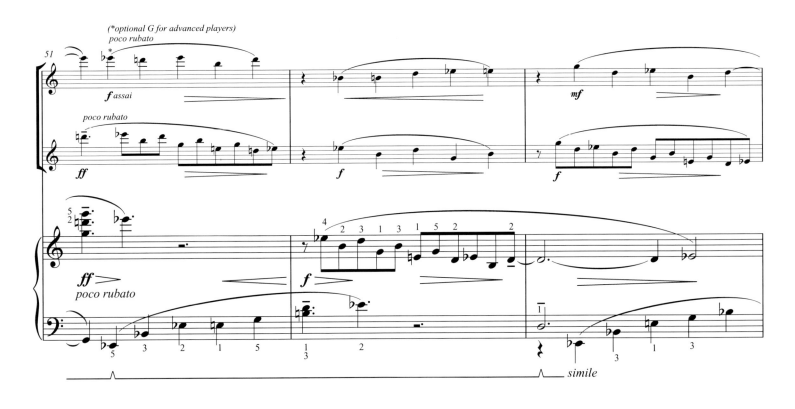

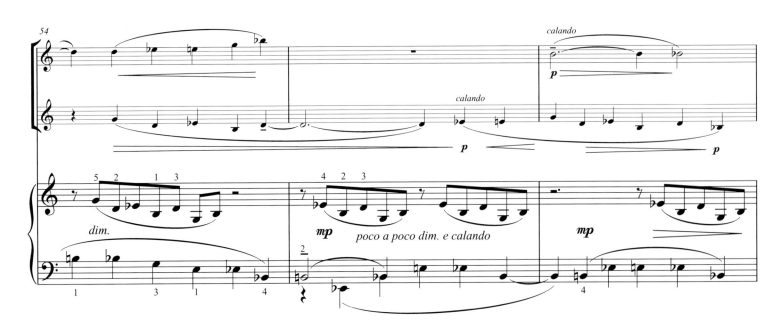

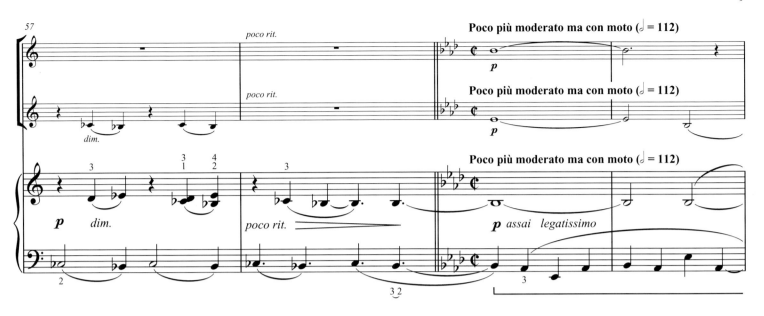

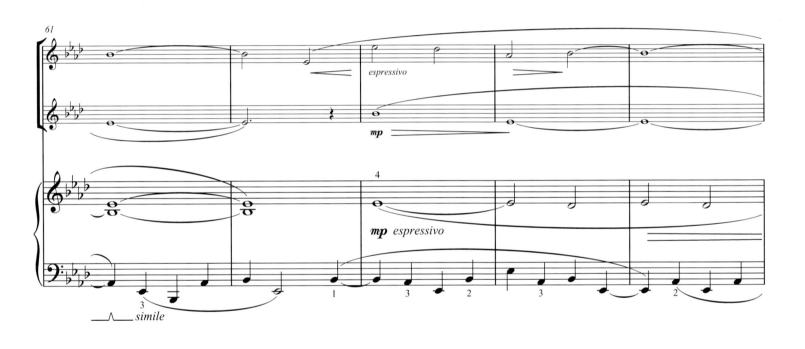

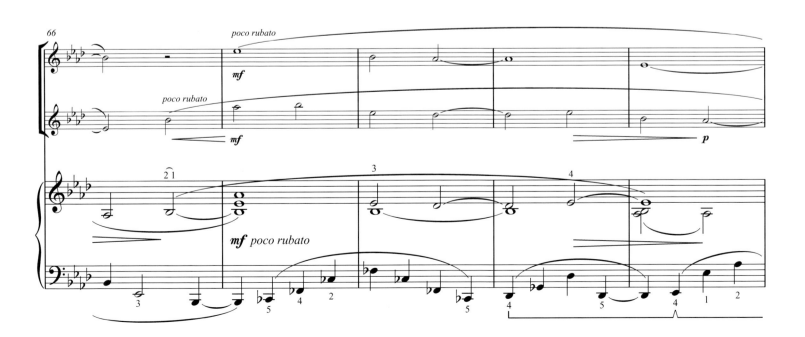

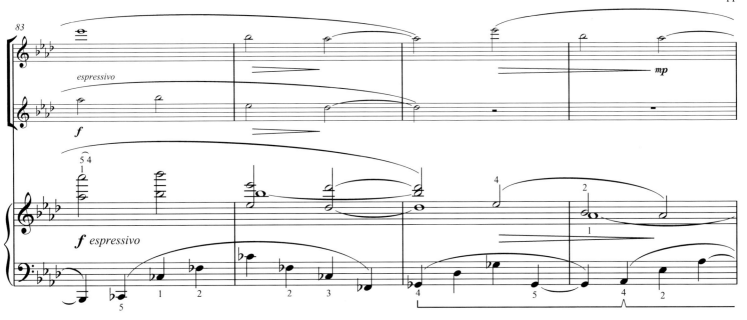

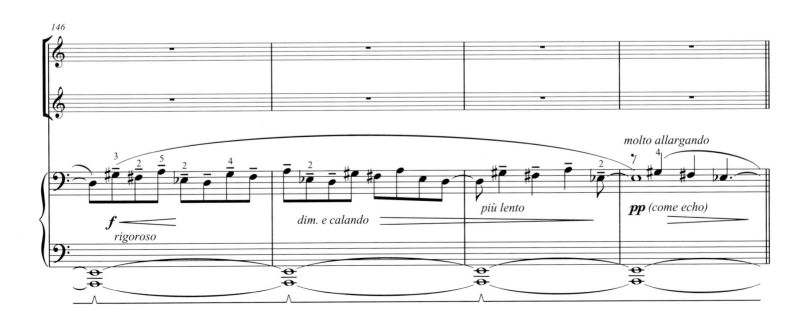

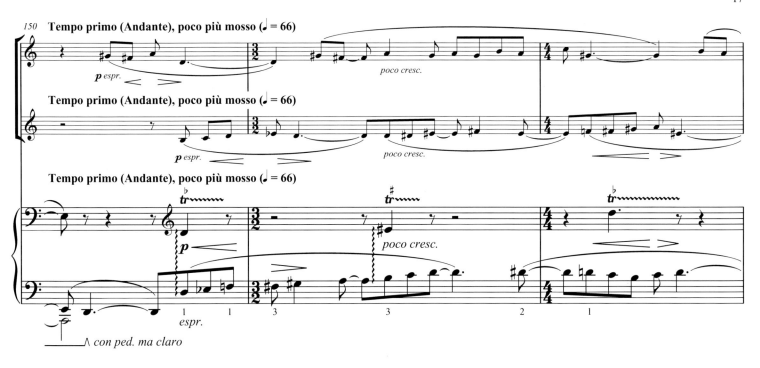

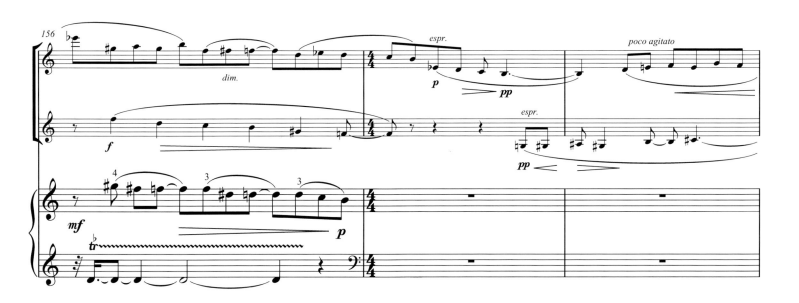

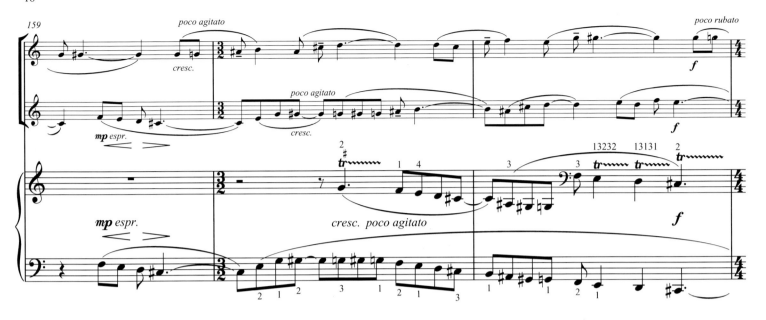

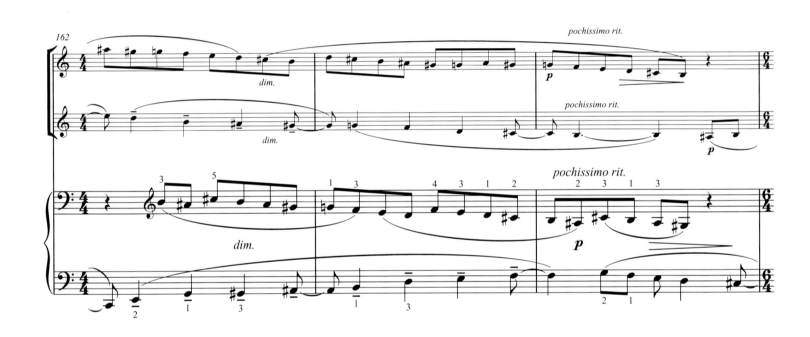

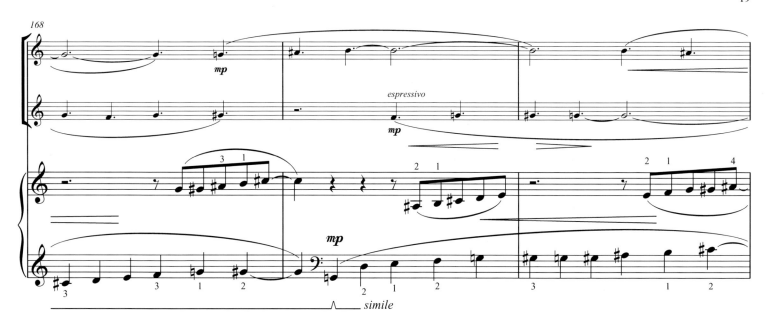

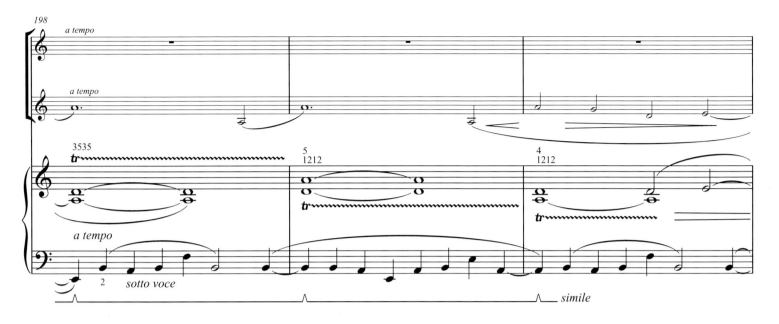

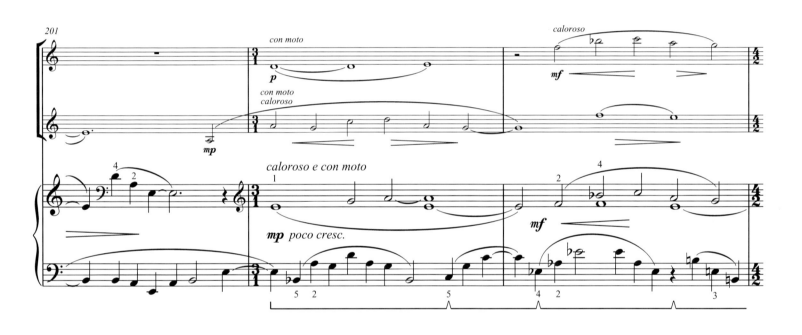

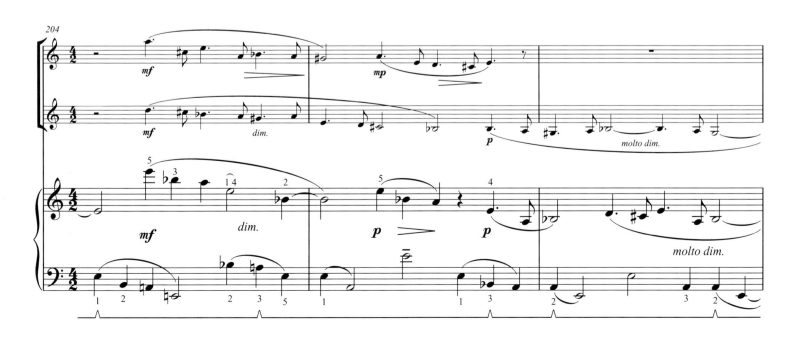

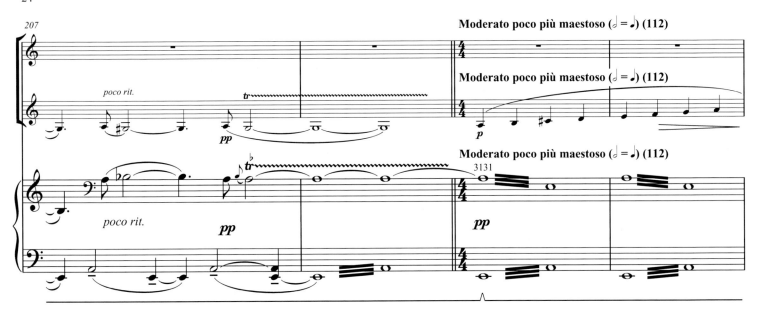

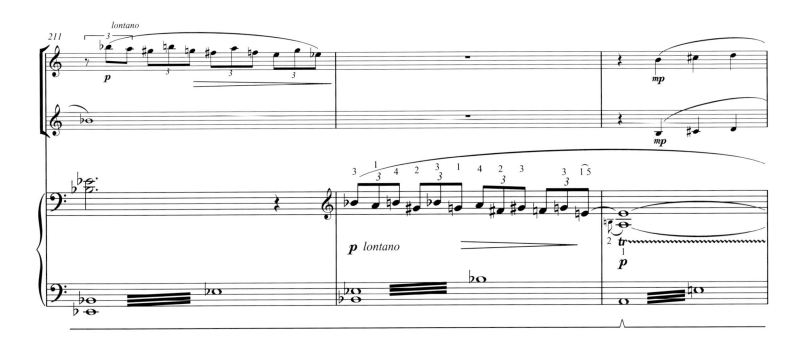

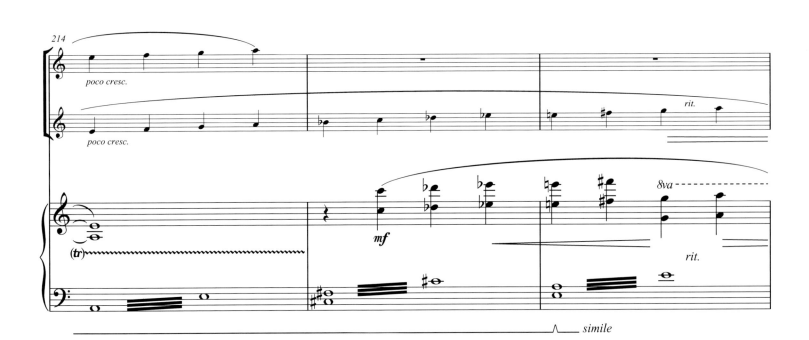

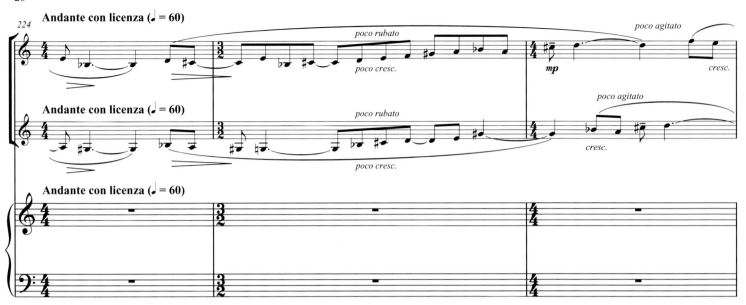

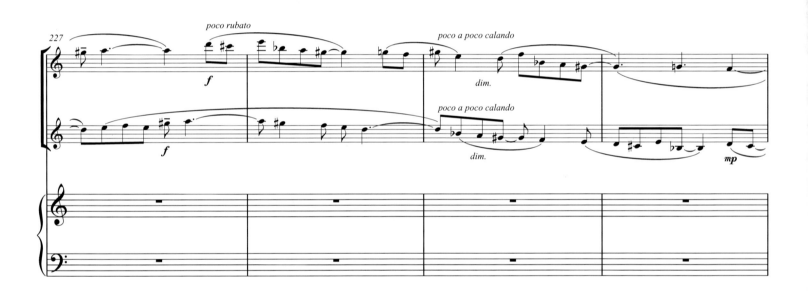

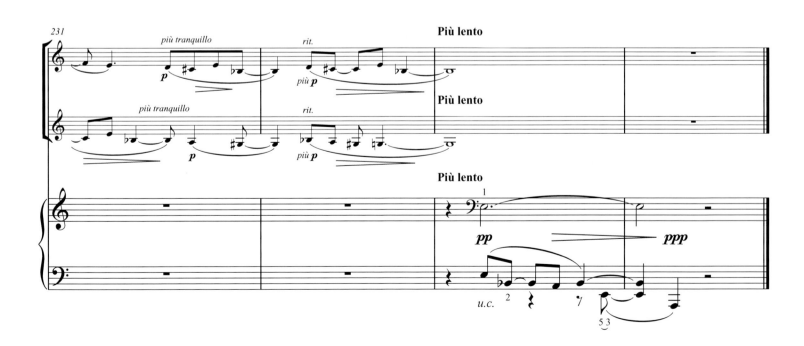

FANTASY

FOR OBOE, B-FLAT CLARINET, AND PIANO
BY CHRISTOS TSITSAROS

OBOE
PART

ISBN 978-1-4950-8442-3

7777 W. BLUEMOUND RD. P.O. BOX 13819 MILWAUKEE, WI 53213

In Australia Contact:
Hal Leonard Australia Pty. Ltd.
4 Lentara Court
Cheltenham, Victoria, 3192 Australia
Email: ausadmin@halleonard.com.au

No part of this publication may be reproduced in any form or by any means without the prior written permission of the Publisher.

Visit Hal Leonard Online at
www.halleonard.com

FANTASY

Oboe

By CHRISTOS TSITSAROS

Copyright © 2017 by HAL LEONARD LLC
International Copyright Secured   All Rights Reserved

Oboe

Oboe

FANTASY

For Oboe, B-Flat Clarinet, and Piano
By Christos Tsitsaros

CLARINET PART

ISBN 978-1-4950-8442-3

HAL•LEONARD®
7777 W. BLUEMOUND RD. P.O. BOX 13819 MILWAUKEE, WI 53213

In Australia Contact:
Hal Leonard Australia Pty. Ltd.
4 Lentara Court
Cheltenham, Victoria, 3192 Australia
Email: ausadmin@halleonard.com.au

No part of this publication may be reproduced in any form or by any means without the prior written permission of the Publisher.

Visit Hal Leonard Online at
www.halleonard.com

FANTASY

Clarinet in B♭

By CHRISTOS TSITSAROS

Copyright © 2017 by HAL LEONARD LLC
International Copyright Secured   All Rights Reserved

Clarinet in B♭